Ray and Paddy

by

Beatrice Sampe

Bloomington, IN  Milton Keynes, UK

authorHOUSE®

AuthorHouse™
1663 Liberty Drive, Suite 200
Bloomington, IN 47403
www.authorhouse.com
Phone: 1-800-839-8640

AuthorHouse™ UK Ltd.
500 Avebury Boulevard
Central Milton Keynes, MK9 2BE
www.authorhouse.co.uk
Phone: 08001974150

First published by AuthorHouse 1/4/2008

ISBN: 978-1-4259-6969-1 (sc)
ISBN: 9781-4259-6969-1 (sc)

Printed in the United States of America
Bloomington, Indiana

This book is printed on acid-free paper.

CHAPTER ONE
RAY'S DREAM -- A PONY OF HIS OWN

Ray sat with his father on the back steps of their white clapboard farm house, resting and warming themselves in the sun. The cold fall wind swirled painted leaves around them. They, along with older brother Billy, had just finished picking apples and storing them in the fruit cellar. The apples would be sorted later, with some packaged for sale and the rest kept for Ray's mom to preserve.

Teddy, their cattle dog of mixed collie breed lay at their feet, warming himself too, and waiting patiently for the command to "Get the cows." With these words he would be off down the road to a yonder field to round up the cows and move them efficiently through the gate and down the road to the barn. Teddy stayed constantly with either Ray or Billy whenever they were outside.

Ray thought about how Mom and his little sister Beaty worked in the hot kitchen all summer long, making jams and jellies from the berry bushes, preserving pears, plum sauce, applesauce and cherries for pie. In addition they picked lettuce, beets, carrots, cucumbers and sweet corn to sell on their Saturday egg route. The Great Depression was upon them and Ray knew his job was to help the family. He wondered if he dare tell Dad his dream.

Just like that a sudden excitement rose up within him. He was alone with Dad now and their short rest would soon be over. Ray cleared his throat and hesitantly said, "Dad, do you think I could ever have a pony? You know how much I like horses. If I could have one, I would take care of him and work even harder to help make money to pay for him."

Dad chuckled. "Now Ray, just how do you think you could make money? Every cent we have must be spent wisely. First of all, if we could scrape a little together, your Mom and I promised Billy a bicycle. He has grown big and strong, has worked hard and deserves one and he is 12 years old already. But it's interesting you should ask about a pony now. I visited with Mr. Brandt, the carnival man, last summer and we actually talked about the possibility of boarding one of his ponies for the winter."

Ray's big blue eyes got even bigger above his freckled rosy cheeks. He grabbed Dad's arm. "Oh Dad! Could we?" Then just a little quieter he repeated, "Could we?"

"Calm down now," Dad said. "First of all we have to find out if the offer is still good. Secondly, we would have to remodel the extra horse stall so a pony could eat from the manger."

"Dad, I think we can handle it. Let's go and see the ponies right now!" Ray grinned with excitement.

Dad grinned too and jumped up. "I'll give him a call... we have time if he has."

Sure enough, Mr. Brandt said for them to come right over. His farm was not far from the Sampe family's farm. As they pulled into Mr. Brandt's yard, Ray's nose up against the car window, he yelled, "Geez Dad, look at all those ponies...and even little colts."

With all the exuberance of a young colt, Ray bounded out of the car and jumped almost to the top of the fence, scaring some of them. But a confident, all-black male hardly moved at all, stared at Ray and then took off, galloping around the field. He ended his performance in front of Ray with his ears forward, as if to say, "Who are you? I think I might like you." Ray noticed his Dad and Mr. Brandt grinning. He burst out, "Dad this is the one I want!"

Dad corrected him gently. "That's the one you want for the winter."

"Ray, I can see why you would pick that pony," Mr. Brandt said. "But watch him now. He is very independant, takes up his space and then some." Sure enough, the black pony nuzzled his nose into a clump of hay the other ponies were eating and a moment later squeezed his way into a space by the water trough.

Ray turned to Dad and Mr. Brandt. "That is the pony I want...for the winter and hopefully forever." He smiled.

"Here's the deal, Fred and Ray," Mr. Brandt said. "You will board him until May of next year and early in the spring I will check to see how you are doing. A bridle and saddle come with the pony. Ray, you are to try and break him in for carnival riding. But be careful! He is very spirited and might show you a thing or two about training," Mr. Brandt warned.

Ray, undaunted by these words, said, "When can you deliver him to our farm?"

Mr. Brandt laughed. "How about tomorrow afternoon?"

Ray looked up at his Dad with big eyes, wondering, "Can we get the stall ready by then?" Dad, after some "aahing" and "urhing," answered, "Yah, ah...how about late afternoon?"

So the agreement was made and as they drove away, Ray craned his neck to watch the black pony as long as he could.

That night at the dinner table, Dad told the plans to board a pony Ray had picked out from Brandt's pony farm. Ray watched his Mom nod approvingly saying, "This can be something for all the children." Little sister Beaty clapped her hands. For her, Ray knew, anything new on the farm was fun. Everyone appeared excited except Billy. His older brother scowled at him.

Suddenly, Ray knew why. Billy was twelve and had

been promised a bike in the spring. Ray was ten, and he was getting his pony first.

When the boys went to bed that night in their shared room, Ray felt that anything about the pony was best left unsaid. But Billy was too upset to keep quiet. "It just isn't fair that the pony is coming before I get my bike."

Ray tried to think of something to say that would make Billy accept the family decision. "Remember, we don't get to keep the pony. When you get your bike, that's forever. And the pony won't cost much money. We just need a few boards for the stall gate, and the little bit of food he will eat."

Billy grumbled, "It's still not fair." With that comment, he rolled over and went to sleep.

CHAPTER TWO
A COLT JOINS THE FAMILY

The next morning while eating breakfast, Dad looked at Ray and Billy. "Boys, we have got our work cut out for us this morning. We have to fix up the horse stall so our new arrival will feel comfortable." He smiled at both of them.

Ray's eyes lit up with anticipation. He responded with a smile of his own, turned to Billy and said teasingly, "Come on Billy, hurry up and finish your breakfast. You know how you like to hammer and saw."

Billy rose slowly from his chair with a groan and a pained look, making sure Ray noticed.

In the barn, Dad issued the orders. "Billy, get the boards I set against the wall in the garage.

To Ray, he said, "you can get the saw, drill, three big metal hinges and the nut and bolt box on the work table. Oh, I almost forgot, there is a big slide bolt lock there, bring that too."

As soon as Billy returned with the boards, Dad laid them out on the floor. He made big black dots with a carpenter's pencil and said, "Billy, you drill holes where I have marked."

7

Ray stood and watched as Dad marked spots on both sides of the stall. "Ray," he said, "pound in a nail to make a little hole, then lay the hinge flange over it and use these flat-head screws to attach the hinges. Be sure to get them all the way into the wood, so they will hold the gate securely.

"I'll work on lowering the manger so the pony can reach his food easily," Dad said with a smile.

Billy and Ray, like most of their friends, enjoyed work like this. They even smiled at each other once in awhile as they worked. Soon the boards looked like a gate, and the gate was ready to mount. The boys held it up so Dad could attach the hinges. The final touch was the slide bolt. When it was installed, all three stood with their hands on their hips, admiring their work.

At almost the same moment, Ray heard the sound of a truck in the yard. He excitedly peeked out the window and yelled, "The pony is here!"

Mr. Brandt drove up in front of the horse barn. As he pulled the trailer ramp down, Mom and Beaty came from the house, excited and smiling. Ray peered through the slats of the trailer to get a glimpse of the pony.

"Hold your horses, Ray! Give the pony some time to come down the ramp and look at his new surroundings," warned Mr. Brandt.

The skittish black pony stepped off the ramp and

pranced around as Mr. Brandt held his halter tightly. His ears were back, eyes darting, and he shook his head to show that he was frightened. Mr. Brandt talked softly to the pony and petted his nose and neck, saying, "we'll give you a little time to settle down...there, there now."

Ray took a step closer and the pony turned and stared at him, ears just a little forward. Ray took a couple more steps smiling, and Mr. Brandt handed Ray the rope. "Talk to him in soft tones and then touch him slowly on his nose and neck."

Just like that, the pony's ears came all the way forward, the frightened look in his eyes softened and he nudged closer to Ray. Ray had a feeling that he and the pony would get along very well.

Çould this pony really like me in such a short time, he wondered.

Mom had to restrain Beaty from jumping around with excitement while everyone smiled in approval...everyone except Billy. He stood back, wearing a frown.

"Now," Mr. Brandt said, looking at Ray. "Grab the lead rope near the halter, tug on it a little bit and say 'giddy-up' or whatever your signal is to move him, and see if he will walk with you."

Ray said, "Giddy-up," with a little tug. The pony began to walk at his side around the yard. "Gee," he said, "this is easy." Ray was so pleased that his very first command to the new pony brought an immediate and correct response.

"Now, encourage him to run at your side," ordered Mr. Brandt. "Good, good!" he said as again the pony and Ray seemed to move as one. The pony held his head high as he trotted. "A sign of good breeding," Mr. Brandt boasted teasingly.

The pony's trotting gait had a definite sound of "piddy-pat," Ray thought. "Did you hear that? That sounds like 'piddy-pat," he remarked to the assembled group. "I think we will call him Paddy because of that sound."

"Paddy it is then," agreed Mr. Brandt. He removed a brand new western leather saddle and bridle from his truck. "You have got to have the best for such a special pony! Now I have to go, so I will check in midwinter by phone to see how everything is going and will return in the spring."

Smiling at Ray, he added, "We'll see what kind of pony trainer you are." He turned to the family. "I think you'll all enjoy Paddy and I'm glad that I could share him with you."

Everyone waved good-bye to Mr. Brandt as he drove out of the yard--even Billy.

Ray immediately returned to leading Paddy around the yard, stopping and starting with commands of "Giddy-up" and "Whoa." Paddy cooperated every time. After each stop, Ray rewarded him by petting him and softly saying,

"Good boy...good boy."

"Hey Ray," Billy called. "Let's see what Paddy thinks of his new stall."

So into the barn they all went. Ray had laid down a nice bed of straw. Paddy entered the stall, ignored the straw and immediately checked out his manger. Ray beamed, removing the lead rope. "Yah Paddy, check out this manger; hay here, water here and ...a nice box with oats over here."

Paddy sniffed lightly at the straw bedding and the hay. He took a little drink and then smelled the oats. "Look Dad, Ray said excitedly, "Paddy is gulping down the oats like there is no tomorrow!"

"That's good," responded Dad, "cuz we got lots in the granary."

Day after day, Ray looked forward to spending time with Paddy. He always brought a treat, like a carrot, apple or sugar lump in his pocket. Soon Paddy learned to expect treats whenever Ray came. He began greeting Ray by nudging his nose into Ray's pockets, shoving him around in the stall, with Ray laughing and loving every minute.

CHAPTER THREE
PADDY'S CURIOSITY GETS THE BEST OF HIM

One winter morning as Ray approached the horse barn, he didn't hear Paddy call his usual "Good morning" whinny. When he opened the barn door, he noticed Paddy's gate was open. Much to Ray's surprise, Paddy wasn't in his stall. Ray called, "Paddy! Paddy! Where are you?" There was no response. Then he heard a weird snorting noise coming from the alleyway that separated the cows and horses. Sure enough, halfway down the alley, there was Paddy leaning against a stall, breathing hard.

"Look at your stomach ... it's so big!" Ray exclaimed. "Paddy, what have you done?"

Paddy staggered up to Ray. That was when Ray saw oats in his nostrils and oats on his whiskers. He was even drooling oats.

Ray shot out of the barn, his feet hardly touching the ground.

"Dad! Come quick," he called as he rushed into the house. "Paddy is sick! He...he...got out of his stall somehow, went down the alley and found the oats barrel. I think he ate too much oats! His stomach is real big and he can hardly

breathe or walk. He looks like he might burst! Oh Dad, he won't die will he?"

Dad ran almost as fast as Ray back to the barn. The minute he saw the pony he said, "Paddy is in deep trouble. Too much oats can cause too much gas to form, which can harm Paddy's insides."

Ray swayed a little and leaned on Dad. "Dad, don't let him die," he wailed. "Do something please!"

"Get the lead rope quick," Dad ordered, "and I will help him out of the barn. If his legs start to buckle, I'll have to hold him up. Then when we get outside, we'll see if he can walk with you on the lead rope. If he can, you will walk him until he relieves himself of all the gas in his stomach. With the mess and smell that he's going to make, I don't want him in the barn!"

Ray looked at Dad quizzically, not knowing quite what to think. "How long will that take?"

"I don't know. He is a very healthy pony, so hopefully not too long. The important thing is to walk, walk, walk. By all means, don't let him lie down. The gas will press on his lungs and heart and he could die," warned Dad. Ray, frightened half out of his wits, took the rope firmly.

"Come on, Paddy, this rope is made for walking, and walking it shall be."

"Yell to me if he should falter and want to lie down," Dad warned Ray. If it comes to that we'll have to hold him up."

He walked when Ray led him, although Paddy staggered a bit. So pony and boy paraded round and round the yard. Soon a terrible aroma and noise filled the air as Paddy released his gas and a trail ran behind Paddy as they walked.

Ray continued to make the circle bigger so he didn't have to step in Paddy's tracks.

"Paddy, how could you do this to yourself?" he asked. "Now look at the mess you're in, and you are not going to stop walking until your belly is smaller, the smell is gone and you stop leaving a trail. Thank goodness it's winter and let's hope it snows to cover this mess up. I don't know if you can smell yourself Paddy, but it's so bad that I have to hold my nose when we go downwind."

Billy soon learned about Paddy's escapade and he couldn't help laughing when he peeked out of the barn. It was a funny sight to watch an exhausted Ray trampling along holding his nose at times when the wind was wrong.

To top it off, Billy just couldn't resist making the most of the moment. He stood there and watched and every time Ray looked at him, he would hold his nose. Then with a big grin he would look skyward and let out a loud, drawn out "Pheeewww!" He got the reaction he wanted...kind of. Ray yelled, "It's not funny! Paddy could have died!"

Billy retorted, "Well he didn't and Dad told me he won't. All I know is that my new bicycle wouldn't cause so much trouble. On top of that, he had the whole family worried."

"You really know how to hurt a guy, don't you?" Ray said.

Later, Dad and Ray investigated the "crime scene." To Ray's surprise Paddy had learned that the slide bolt on the outside of his gate held it shut. With his little snout he was able to slide the bolt back and "Voila"...the gate opened!

"That will be easy to remedy," Dad said. "We'll just attach another board here on the inside that runs well past the slide bolt. Then he can't get anywhere near it with his nose." Ray was relieved the solution was that simple.

By evening Paddy had recovered from his overdose of oats. As Ray put down fresh straw in Paddy's stall, he took Paddy's face and pulled it right up to his. "Don't you ever do such a dumb thing again!"

He looked into Paddy's eyes and Paddy gradually lowered his eyes and head as if in shame. "It makes me feel a little better that I can at least scold you for all the walking we had to do," Ray told him. Then gave him a big hug and said, "But I'm sure glad you're all right."

As Ray headed up to bed that night, Dad put his hand lightly on Ray's shoulder. "Good job Ray."

Ray had time for one thought as his head hit the pillow... training a pony sure was hard work. In seconds he was fast asleep.

CHAPTER FOUR
TRAINING PADDY

After Paddy recovered, Ray knew that the pony's real training had to begin. One winter morning, Ray and Billy walked to the barn together.

"You should see Paddy and me when I get in his stall," Ray said to Billy. "He is so anxious to get the treat I bring him each morning that he shoves me all around the stall. He doesn't give up until he finds the right pocket.

"On top of that he likes it when I curry and brush him. You know he never got attention like that at Mr. Brandt's farm. I think he really likes me." Ray smiled with pleasure.

Sure enough, when Ray entered Paddy's stall, the pony immediately started his search of Ray's pockets, shoving him all around. "Isn't this funny?" said Ray.

Billy answered sarcastically. "I don't see what's so funny. Maybe you think it's funny, but I don't."

Ray felt anger rise. "I wish you would get over the fact that Paddy is here and I'm enjoying him and you don't have your bicycle yet. You know Dad promised it to you, so get over it! And you couldn't ride a bike now anyhow because of the ice and snow."

Later that morning Dad approached Ray. "It's a relatively warm day today. I think we should work with Paddy and see how he accepts the bridle. If he accepts that, we'll try the saddle. If he likes that, maybe even a short ride around the yard with someone on the lead."

Finally, Ray thought as his eyes lit up...this is the day!

The bridle fit Paddy perfectly and he seemed to accept the straps around his head, since they were similar to his halter.

However, the bit that went into his mouth was new and different.

Paddy seemed to want to shove it this way and that. Ray was sure that if he could have spit it out, he would have.

"Do even ponies have to have one of these?" Ray asked. I know it's important for big horses because they are so powerful and you have to have control, but ponies?"

"You'll find the bit is just as important with your Paddy," Dad responded. "By saying "Whoa' and pulling up and back on the reins attached to the big rings, you'll get him to stop because he'll feel a little bit of pain in his mouth. Gradually he will learn that if he stops right away when he hears 'Whoa' there might not be a tug at all and important to Paddy, no pain in his mouth."

Dad gave the reins to Ray. "Lead him around with the two reins in your right hand, held high and back a little, and hold the lead rope in the other. Then try 'whoa' if you like."

Ray wasn't quite tall enough to pull the reins straight up and back, but even so Paddy stopped immediately with Ray's slight tug and the command, "whoa." Easy as pie, Ray thought. He turned and smiled at Dad and Billy.

"Now let's see what Paddy does with the saddle and the two cinch straps around his stomach," said Dad. "This is kind of a tricky maneuver; too tight and the horse won't like it, too loose and the rider and saddle will be under his belly in the wink of an eye. If I know horses, Paddy will not like this part." Dad rolled his eyes and gave a half-grin.

Ray and Billy quickly found an old blanket in the barn that they folded to make a saddle pad, and then on went the saddle. Paddy jumped away a little. "Whoa Paddy," Dad said softly. "This is part of the fun of being a riding pony."

Dad showed Ray how to put the stirrup up over the saddle while he attached the front cinch strap to the rings on the saddle.

"Easy now Paddy," Dad said softly again. "This won't hurt, but it might feel a little uncomfortable."

With Dad's first pull, Paddy jumped up, lifting his front legs. Dad grabbed the reins, jerking on them a little. "Whoa Paddy, calm down now."

Just like that Paddy settled down. Then Dad changed his tactics, asking Ray to hold the reins tightly. Paddy would learn quickly that if he did anything other than what was expected of him, a pull on the bit and a little pain would be the result. Paddy stood still as the first strap was secured.

But when Dad pulled the saddle toward him, it wobbled.

"Aha! I thought Paddy might do that. See, he took a deep breath as I pulled on the strap, which made this area of his stomach much bigger. He also knew enough to hold his breath until I secured the strap. As soon as I let go, he exhaled and sure enough, the strap is loose. See, I can put my hand in here between the strap and his tummy." Dad smiled showing the boys.

"He can't do quite the same thing when you attach the back cinch strap, because his lungs are more to the front of his torso. So always be sure the front strap is as tight as you can make it. Hang onto it when you slip it through the saddle ring, and wait until he exhales to make the final binding.

"Now I want you boys to practice so that when I'm not around you will be able to do it yourselves. I think until he learns to stand perfectly still while being saddled, you better keep the lead rope short and attached to the front of the manger."

The boys practiced over and over again, chuckling as they out-maneuvered Paddy on one of his tricks. They wanted to get on with the big test of the day...riding Paddy.

"Ray, first walk Paddy around a little so he gets used to the feel of the saddle," Dad ordered.

Paddy did this part perfectly, and Ray's eagerness took over. "Please Dad, can I get on now?"

"Okay, let's try it," Dad said, smiling. "Put the reins evenly in your left hand and grab the saddle horn with the same hand. Put your left foot firmly in the stirrup, right hand on the back of the saddle and give a quick 'heave ho,' throwing your right leg over."

Ray carefully gathered the reins, grabbed the saddle horn and put his foot firmly, as Dad had stressed, into the stirrup. It touched Paddy's side, making him move away from Ray. Ray hopped along on one foot. A quick glance at Billy and Ray noticed he had his hand over his mouth with a big grin peeking out the sides of his face.

Dad yelled, "Get your foot out of the stirrup and pull up quickly on the reins to make Paddy understand that he must let you mount! I think we better give you a little help until you both get the hang of it."

Now Dad held the bridle and Ray mounted quickly.

"Okay Ray, you're going to be on your own now. Pull those reins up and back, so he can't get his head down. If he does, it allows Paddy to buck high in the rear. If he comes up in the front, hang on to the horn with one hand so you don't slide off the back. With the other hand push the back of his head down with your reins in that same hand."

Ray thought this was a complicated business. He had no idea that so much went into getting on a horse. On top of that, he had to break this horse for saddle riding.

Slowly, Dad let go of the bridle, and Ray and Paddy did an abbreviated bucking bronco show. Ray wobbled back, forward and even sideways as Paddy tried every move he could. Finally, he got tired of jumping around. "That-a-boy Paddy, we did it!" Ray said. "Let's show 'em now and take a little tour around the yard."

Ray managed this almost as well as a seasoned rider, and Dad beamed with pride that boy and horse bonded so quickly and so well.

"Is it my turn now?" Billy asked. Ray relinquished his seat and held the bridle until Billy got on. Ray, with a mischievous grin, asked, "Are you ready?"

With his first leap, Paddy knew he had a much heavier rider on his back and didn't like it at all. The bucking bronco show rose to new heights. Paddy went up with his front legs, then down and then quickly kicked with both rear legs. Soon Billy was hanging on to the saddle horn with no control of the reins. Once more Paddy's front legs went up and Billy just gave up and slipped off his back to the ground.

Immediately Paddy stopped moving and sniffed Billy. Dad and Ray ran to him, trying not to laugh. "Are you okay?"

Billy replied meekly, "I guess so...ah but I think Paddy doesn't like me."

Ray laughed saying, "That is the understatement of the year."

Dad looked at Ray worriedly. "Let's hope Paddy is not a 'one-rider pony.' Mr. Brandt won't like that." Dad trying to imply to Ray that this was somewhat a serious situation.

"Good!" snapped Billy. "I don't mind a bit if he has to go back!"

CHAPTER FIVE
PONY VS. BIKE

Spring approached and the whole family knew that Mr. Brandt would soon call to see how Paddy's training was coming along.

One evening, sitting at the table after dinner with a cup of coffee, Dad asked the children to excuse themselves from the table indicating that he wanted to discuss something personally with Mom.

Ray and Billy decided to play cards in the living room. Ray suspecting that the conversation in the kitchen would be about Paddy, and perhaps the bike for Billy, Ray positioned himself near the kitchen door.

The boys shuffled and played cards quietly, barely speaking, but then Ray made a quiet signal with his finger to his mouth and lifted his eyes towards the kitchen. He wanted to hear the conversation.

Dad spoke softly. "Nan, I feel that the boys are not getting along very well with each other and most of the problem lies with Paddy."

He added, "Billy has not adjusted to him and is asking almost every day when I will take him to Manitowoc to buy his bike. He has pored over catalogs and ads in the paper night after night and knows exactly what kind of bike he wants.

"The important thing is, I think we have enough money to cover the cost of the bike. Billy has worked hard and waited long enough."

When Dad and Mom's conversation ended, Ray knew what was coming when Dad approached them in the living room.

"Boys, your mother and I have made a decision. Day after next, Billy, you and I will go to Manitowoc and look at bikes. If the price is right and the bike is what you want, it's yours and we'll bring it home."

Billy smiled from ear to ear. He leaped and excitedly said, "Yippee" a couple of times.

Ray looked at him disgustedly. "All right! All right, you can stop jumping now! He turned to Dad. "Could I come along?"

Dad looked at him for a moment with a puzzled expression.

"Not one word out of you, then you can come along," Dad warned.

"Now there is another bit of business that has to be dealt with, involving you, Ray. You know Mr. Brandt will be calling soon. What can we tell him? That Paddy is a bucky little son-of-a-gun and at this point dislikes having any rider on his back but you?"

"We'll keep working on that, Dad. Maybe after Billy gets his bike, he'll smell better to Paddy and Paddy will let him ride. Horses have an inner sense about humans." Ray grinned.

"You better not talk so smart," Billy snapped. "If he won't allow riders, he's got to go back to the pony farm and run around in the fields for the rest of his life."

That night when the boys went to bed, Ray worried about Paddy's refusal to accept riders. Would Mr. Brandt really take him back? Yet he wished so much that Paddy could stay. If Paddy doesn't shape up, Ray thought, Mr. Brandt won't be able to use him this summer, and maybe never. As he drifted off to sleep, he wondered if maybe the family could bargain and buy him somehow.

The next day, Mom and Dad emptied the jar where proceeds from eggs and chickens were kept and carefully counted out twenty dollars. They looked at each other with great relief...enough for a bike.

The very next day Dad, Ray and Billy drove to the bicycle shop in Manitowoc. On arrival, Billy quickly jumped out of the truck. Ray followed and they went immediately to a display of Schwinns. Billy walked up and down the row. Ray became impatient.

"You're taking an awful long time to decide...pick one and let's go!"

The man who owned the store came over to Billy as he pulled a shiny black bike from the rack. "You sure know good quality. That's a Schwinn DX, and it comes with that horn and light. Look at its advanced lines. The paint job is guaranteed and durability is a standard feature for this bike. For twenty dollars you will enjoy it for many years to come." He smiled at Billy.

On the way home the tension between Billy and Ray eased a bit. Billy took the first ride after taking the bike off the truck and rode around for a good long time, enjoying every minute with a big broad grin.

Watching, Ray grew impatient again. "Let me have a turn." He grabbed the handle bars and threw his leg over the seat so hard that he almost lost control. Finally he straightened out and off he went.

"Be careful," Billy yelled, "and don't you dare scratch that bike!"

When Ray got back, Billy issued a challenge. "If you can get your Paddy whipped into shape, we can have some competition like racing down the road...maybe even jumping."

"Maybe," Ray said, smiling to himself. If his family could buy Paddy, he and Billy could have plenty of competitions.

"However," Dad said, "back to the problem at hand, Ray. We have to make Paddy understand that when other riders are on his back, he has to behave himself. That will take some time.

"He seems to recognize immediately when a heavier and bigger rider is in the saddle and doesn't want any part of them. He could be trained for smaller children like Beaty, but you know that as soon as you let go of the lead strap, he darts off in a trot to the orchard and tries to scrape them off under low branches. I would say that with our present progress, he might not be ready for small children until the end of the summer. Shetlands have a mind of their own and are hard to train."

When Mr. Brandt called, Dad invited him to visit the farm to see the progress Paddy had made. To start, Ray showed Mr. Brandt how he had figured out Paddy's trick about the cinch strap when saddling him. Mr. Brandt enjoyed that little scenario and then watched as Ray mounted. Paddy stood very still with ears forward.

"Watch, said Ray. "I don't even have to nudge him or anything. He responds to my 'giddy-up' immediately." Off they went in a pleasant slow trot.

Ray called back to his audience, "Watch now. With just a little nudge with my feet and Paddy will go into a fast gallup." It was a pleasant sight to see, rider and pony as one.

"I'm very impressed, Ray. That's good work for the short time you had," said Mr. Brandt. "Now let's see what Paddy does with other kids."

"Ah..." said Ray. "We only tried Billy and Beaty and we weren't very successful," he admitted.

"Let me see how Paddy acts with Billy on his back," requested Mr. Brandt.

Billy stepped forward with eyebrows raised to the sky. As he gathered the reins and put his foot into the stirrup to mount, Paddy did his evasive dance to perfection. Poor Billy hopped along on one foot for some distance and then with a great heave-ho hoisted himself into the saddle.

At the same time Billy tried to tighten the reins, Paddy made his first big bucking leap with his head down. Billy almost tumbled over Paddy's head. In another split second, Paddy made a weird squeal, raised high in the front and Billy had to grab for the saddle horn so he would't slide off the back. As Mr. Brandt and Dad attempted to grab the reins, Paddy darted to the side and took off in one of his wildest gallops.

At this point, Teddy couldn't help but get excited about the out-of-control pony and rider. With Billy yelling "whoa" and hanging onto the saddle horn, Teddy decided to join the chase, barking at Paddy's heels.

"Geez Dad," Ray said. "Teddy is doing the wrong thing. He's only making Paddy run faster."

Ray added, I'm going to try to call Teddy off and hope Billy can hang on until Paddy stops."

Ray called to Teddy, loudly several times. "Teddy come here!" As Teddy heard Ray calling, he quickly returned to

Ray's side and sat thinking he would get a good pet and verbal compliment. Ray looked down at Teddy and said sternly, "Teddy, we didn't need that performance from you, Paddy was going fast enough." With that comment, Teddy dejectedly put his head down and laid at Ray's feet.

Finally Paddy must have felt that he had put on a good show and gradually slowed and trotted towards the group.

Dad looked at Mr. Brandt. Chuckling he said, "Thank goodness the yard gate was closed or who knows where Billy and Paddy would have wound up."

After Paddy stopped, Billy, his face ashen, slowly slid out of the saddle and staggered to the side. "I'm not going to help anymore with training that pony!"

Mr. Brandt looked at Paddy and then at Dad and Ray and said, "Some Shetlands have an independent nature and are very hard to train. Mr. Brandt looked away and then turned to Ray and said, "...and he is such an excellent Shetland specimen too. Things look pretty bleak for Paddy to be ready by Carnival time."

Ray stood silently and listened. Suddenly he stepped forward, squared his shoulders and said, "Could we buy him? How much do you want?"

Dad rocked back, eyebrows raised. Mr. Brandt countered quickly. "Fifty dollars including bridle and saddle."

Ray was still thinking. "Could we pay you half, like

twenty-five down and the other twenty-five after the crops come in, in the fall?"

With Ray's comment, Dad tried to regain his composure. Looking at Mr. Brandt, he said, "I realize these are hard times for everyone, but would you give us time to talk this over as a family? That is, if you would consider twenty-five down and the balance in the fall?"

Mr. Brandt smiled at Ray. "I can wait a few days for your decision."

"I guess we'll have to have a family meeting very quickly," commented Dad. "We have to figure out where the first half of the payment will come from. Then, how we can add the other twenty- five dollars in the fall. Remember, our pockets are pretty empty after buying the bicycle."

Both scared and hopeful, Ray followed Dad and Billy toward the house.

CHAPTER SIX
THE FAMILY MEETING

That evening after all the chores were done, all five Sampes sat down at the kitchen table to decide whether Paddy stayed.

"As I said before, we could make more money this summer just from the farm itself...if we all work hard,' Ray said enthusiastically.

Ray looked at Billy. He knew this was where any negative vote would come from. "Remember the old chicken coop near the orchard. We could patch that up a little bit. That's right down your alley, Billy. Then we order double the usual number of baby chicks. When they are heavy enough to be fryers we'll sell half of them and the rest we'll keep for laying hens. I'll take care of them just as I have in the past."

Continuing, Ray offered an idea for the whole family. "There is plenty of space near the orchard to make the garden bigger. We could let the city people on our weekly egg route know that we have vegetables and fruit for sale too."

"Dad and I also talked about something else," Mom said. "What do you think about us raising a couple of pigs for meat on our table? We have room in the barn, and in the fall that would reduce our grocery bill quite a bit."

Ray stopped chewing. "I like the idea of eating more pork chops and stuff, but I've been in barns where they raise pigs. As far as I'm concerned, pigs stink."

"I tend to agree with Ray, Mom," Billy added. "On top of that I suppose cleaning out the pen will be our work, right Dad?"

"Well, we'll set the pen separate from the other animals on the barn floor and it will only be a temporary thing. Yes, cleaning the pen will be your work. I feel we have the room, and by winter they will be gone...off to the butcher shop."

Ray looked at Billy, then turned to Mom and Dad. "I think you have already made up your minds about the pigs. I guess we could try it, right Billy?"

Beaty had been listening quietly to the suggestions and finally piped up. "Let's get back to that bigger garden business. I see now that Ray is pulling me into this work, Mom and I did lots of hoeing and picking last year and that's hard work."

"You won't be overworked," Mom assured Beaty quickly. "I'm sure the boys will help when they can."

"Yah!" Billy said with a scowl. "After working all day on the crops, milking amd evening chores, including the pigs, you think we'll want to hoe until dark?"

"Now, now Billy," Dad said. "We don't want to get into an argument about this. Ray's and Mom's suggestions are valid ones and I have another."

"The county fair is coming up in Åugust and in the past we had only a minimum of entries. Why don't we add a few more...like chickens, vegetables and Mom's baked and canned goods? At a dollar a piece for first prize, that would add up.

"I was also approached last year at the fair about being the poultry house supervisor for fair week this year. The pay is good. I think I could spend those days away from the farm. If Paddy stays, I will notify the Fair Board right away that I'm available."

Ray had never thought of that little extra, and a huge smile grew on his freckled face.

Mom spoke again. "We can be more diligent in spraying and caring for the orchard, and make sure that the fruit from all the different trees will be picked when ripe and be of good quality. I'm sure the city folk will take a good amount of fresh produce off our hands, and even pick what they want when they visit. We could use our Paddy as an asset. Maybe Paddy will be trained by then. With Beaty leading him, he might allow the children a nice ride."

Billy said quickly, "That's the biggest 'MAYBE' I ever heard. Paddy is the buckiest and contrary animal I've ever witnessed."

He continued, leaning his head on his hand as if overworked already.

"I'm sitting here thinking about all the added work and it appears I'm going to be involved in about four more chores. I hope I have time to ride my bike. I don't know any other kids that work as hard as we're going to work."

"It's only going to be for one summer," Ray said. "You can slack off after that."

"And where are we going to get the twenty-five dollars for the down payment?" Billy asked sarcastically.

"I was coming to that," Dad said slowly. We had a good summer last year and have extra grain and hay. We can sell that and I'm sure we can get twenty-five dollars for it."

Billy rose from the table. "You better be ready to work your fanny off, Ray."

"Now, now," Mom said sternly, "We'll have none of that! We are in this together and I'm sure the end result will be that all three of you will eventually enjoy Paddy. And not only that, don't forget the visiting families. The children can't all ride at once, so maybe some will play with you or will help their parents gather their own produce."

So that seemed to end the meeting and Dad called Mr. Brandt and he was happy that it all worked out for the family.

As Ray crawled into bed, he said to himself, "Paddy is half mine, thank you God." That night he dreamed of galloping with Paddy over the fields and a break-neck speed race with Billy and his bike.

Spring arrived with all its warmth and beauty. Along with the mother cows giving birth to their calves, two cute little pink piglets arrived and were placed in their pen. They seemed to enjoy their new surroundings along with Beaty feeding them their necessary ground feed and old apples and carrots.

Ray reminded Dad to order the baby chicks from the hatchery. Soon thereafter Dad and Ray arrived at the kitchen door with two big flat boxes. "Here they are Beaty! We'll put them near the wood stove to keep them warm until we put the finishing touches on the chicken coops," Dad said with a big smile.

Beaty jumped up and down and Ray watched Beaty's eyes get big when Dad opened the boxes. Peep holes were along the sides and every now and then a little beak would try to peek out. As the cover came off there they were, a mass of yellow fluff balls, chirping away and tumbling over each other. Ray and Dad grinned as they watched Beaty's fascination with the little chicks.

"Oh!" "Oh!" Beaty cried. "How small and cuddly they are. Can I hold one?"

"Yes," said Mom, "but now be very careful. Don't squeeze them. They can suffocate in the boxes or in their coops if they are frightened or cold and push against each other."

Ray added. "Remember we paid for each one, something like twenty-five cents per chick."

"Okay," Beaty said. She peeked through the little peepholes, stuck her finger through and watched them turn their little heads and peck lightly. Then she picked one up.

"Easy now," Ray said. "You heard what Mom said."

When the little fluff ball got into her hands, it became very frightened and fluttered its wings.

"No! No!" exclaimed Beaty as she took a firmer grip so the little chick would not fall to the floor. Just like that, the chick's head went to the side, its dark eyes closed, and it lay limp in her hands.

"Oh my gosh! What have I done? Oh Mom, I didn't mean to do it, but I was afraid it would fall. Can you make it wake up?" Beaty whimpered.

"No, I'm afraid not, and I know that you didn't mean to do it," Mom said. "I think the hatchery always gives customers an extra couple chicks. Sometimes they suffocate just from being placed in the box, so if we only lose one, it's bad but not the end of the world. However, I think you learned a valuable lesson and that's important."

Ray felt disgusted. "Geez Beaty, Mom even warned you and you still managed to suffocate the first one you held. Do you realize that we had to pay twenty-five cents for each chick? Listen...from here on keep your hands out of the boxes and off the chicks!

After a day, the coops were ready, furnished with hooded heater lamps, feeding fountains and mash troughs. Ray laid lots of soft straw on the floor and the little chicks adapted well to their new home. Beaty visited often, laughing at a few that accidentally would slip into the water trough of the fountain. They evidently did not like their impromptu baths as they would shake their little bodies and flutter their wings for sometime to get dry. Beaty also tried to help Ray wash and refill their feeders. Ray reminded her that if she noticed that either hooded heat lamp was out, that she must come and tell either himself or Dad right away.

Ray was anxious to get the garden started and the whole family, even Billy pitched in. Ray was so pleased that Dad used his work horses to prepare the soil. Long twine was stretched between stakes, with Billy making a small furrow along the twine. Ray and Beaty dropped the seeds precisely as the packets described. Then Billy followed up with a garden rake, gently covering the seeds. The empty packets were placed on the stakes, so when the little green leaves poked through the ground they would know exactly what vegetable it was.

All five stood together, smiling and admiring their work. "Just a little light rain will get the seeds atarted and then watch the garden grow," Dad remarked. For the first time, Ray and Billy took an interest in the garden.

He turned to the boys and said, "Remember, I said that tools used, must be cleaned and stored in their regular place when work is done so we can find them the next time we want to use them.

The boys picked up hoes, rakes, and left-over marking sticks, trudging along slowly as they were so tired. Ray looked at Billy and said "Will Dad ever just once let us put them away tomorrow?"

"I heard that comment," Dad said. "I know you are tired and all, but if tools are cared for properly, they can be used for years and still look like new."

"Well, there's our lesson for today," muttered Billy, turning away from Dad so he wouldn't hear.

"Ray and Billy," Beaty realizing how much they hated to clean up, said, "If you clean them under the pump, I'm sure Dad will give me his old crank-case oil pail and his big brush. I'll put the oil on the hoes and rakes for you...I like to do that. It's almost like painting and he let me oil his big plow once."

Ray and Billy looked at each other and raised their eyebrows.

"At least she can help a little," Ray said smirking.

CHAPTER SEVEN
SUMMER'S WORK

As the hot summer days approached, everything seemed to fall into place. The garden thrived under the care of Mom and Beaty. The abundant hay crop was ready to be brought in to the barn for winter feed.

One evening Dad announced to the boys, "Better get to bed early tonight. Tomorrow, right after morning chores we will be bringing in the hay that is cut and in rows out in the field. Ray, we need you to drive the horses on the wagon as we load in the field and unload in the barn."

"Billy, you will help stack the hay on the wagon in the field. When we get back to the barn, you will stick the big fork which lifts the hay into the mow. I will spread it in the mow.

"Both of you must follow my calls and directions carefully so no one gets hurt. Ray, by driving horses on the forklift, you are moved into Billy's old slot and you won't have to pull rope anymore. Maybe Beaty, you might do that." Dad looked at her and smiled.

Ray laughed. Mocking a woman's voice, he said sweetly, "You won't mind doing my old job, will you?"

Beaty lifted her nose in the air. "If I have time between weeding and hoeing in the BIG garden."

Ray beamed at the thought that he would drive the big horses.

Finally, he thought, he had an important job.

The next morning they were off to the hay field. Ray had a good command of the horses as they loaded the field hay into the big wagon. When they got back to the barn to unload, he had to quickly unhitch the horses from the wagon and attach them to a crossbar which was attached to a very long rope. This rope passed through a series of pulleys inside the barn and appeared directly above the wagon with the giant fork.

Ray waited for Billy's signal that he had placed the fork with the big tines and was ready for the lift. As Ray started the horses, the rope would tighten on the fork pulley and the tines would grip forcefully into a big clump of hay. Gradually the whole clump would rise to the ceiling. There it joined a gear slide that would send it along to the mow. When it was in just the right spot, Dad would yell "whoa" very loudly. That was the signal for Billy to pull the trip rope attached to the fork. Down the hay would fall with a gentle swish near Dad. Billy talked about how scary that was for him, hoping that the fork full of hay didn't bury Dad. They agreed that Dad would call "okay" very loudly so Billy could start pulling the fork back. Also Ray had to rein in the horses immediately to stop the progress of the hay speeding along the track at the top of the barn.

Ray talked with Dad about his horse driving duties. "When I start the horses to pull the hay into the mow, the rope attached to the crossbar behind the horses quivers and shakes due to the weight of the forkload. The horses really pull hard, leaning forward digging their hooves into the dirt and gravel.

"I look at that taut rope every now and then 'cuz I think if that rope breaks, I will go flying across the yard with the horses. Also, what about Billy? He watches the forkload go up and doesn't really think about where he is standing. If the rope breaks or the fork for some reason lets loose, the hay will fall on top of him. He could get hurt."

Dad reassured Ray, "I always check every inch of that rope to be sure it's as strong as can be. I make sure every pulley is secure in its moorings and every knot on the forklift as well."

With Dad's explanation and reassuring smile, Ray felt a lot better about his new job.

The boys and Dad made many trips from the hay field to the barn. Finally the hay was in the barn ready for winter feed. Ray never counted the number of trips, but he was glad when the work was done.

Now there was more work with the chickens. The two chicken coops had been moved to a nearby field. There the chickens could free range, giving them exposure to fresh air and sun as they enjoyed searching for bugs and seeds. The proud roosters strutted among the hens, sporting their pure white feathers and bright red combs.

Ray and Dad talked about the chickens and the need to separate them. Dad agreed that it was time, and he would make some calls about the fryers to past customers, banquet halls and meat markets. Ray was thrilled to think he'd soon have some real money from his chickens.

That very next day, Ray was up at the crack of dawn. He whistled as he strolled through the dew-covered grass towards the coops. As he approached, he noticed some chickens on the ground outside the coop. That's funny, he thought. Why and how did those chickens get out of the coop? As he got closer, he saw other chickens floundering in the deep grass, unable to get up. Breaking into a run, he reached the coop to find a horrible sight. Dead chickens lay there, half eaten, and many live ones were maimed and bloody. Ray sagged against the coop trying not to throw up.

Tears almost blinding him as he turned and ran, screaming as loud as he could, "Dad! Dad! Wake up! Wake up!"

Ray burst into the house still screaming. Dad leaned sleepily over the stair railing. "What on earth are you yelling about so early in the morning?"

"Dad you have to come right away. Something got into the chicken coop and killed--or half killed--all the

chickens! Come quick--some are bleeding to death. What are we going to do?"

Soon the whole household was up, dressed hurriedly and rushed out to the coops. Mom said, "Fred, I'm going back to the house with Beaty. I don't particularly want her to remember this carnage. We'll talk more about it at breakfast. I think Billy should come with us and he can start milking the cows."

As Dad and Ray dejectedly walked around the coops, Ray noticed that one coop was intact. The chickens inside were anxious to get out to feed and roam for the day. Ray turned to Dad, "Thank goodness these chickens are okay."

"Thank goodness is right," replied Dad. "Now looking at all of this, I'm sure it was foxes. They just pushed in the window and the killing began.

"We have to get to work now. Pile the dead ones here and the ones that have maimed wings or legs, place carefully in the crate behind the coop. Those we can salvage with Mom's help. It's a gory job, but things like this happen."

"Yah," Ray mumbling thoughtfully, "but why us?" As he piled the dead and put the injured chickens in the crate... he felt it was the worse job he had ever been asked to do. It was hard not to up-chuck right on top of the poor birds. He didn't say anymore, as he knew that Dad felt as bad as he did.

After a little while, Dad noticed Ray's expression. "Ray, you've done enough here, I'll finish. I'll feed the other chickens and let them out.

"Now that this happened, we'll have to cull the chickens later in the day. The laying hens will be safe in the laying pens near the house. I'll make sure the other coop is secure for the chickens that are left for the short time we have before we sell them."

At breakfast the family was very quiet until Ray raised his teary eyes from his cereal. "How many do you think we lost, Dad?"

Dad looked at Ray with pain in his own face also. "Well, I think maybe half. We could break even, but our projected profit is gone. We'll just have to make a greater effort on our other summer projects."

Billy and Ray noticed the two little "porkers" were growing fast and stretching their legs by chasing each other around the pen. Beaty, liking all baby animals, spent many hours watching them. She brought nonsaleable garden vegetables and threw them in the pigs' trough. Beaty laughed as they pushed each other around to get the most. Ray walked by one day and said, "Keep feeding them...the bigger they get, the sooner they go."

As days wore on, Ray worked even harder then before and felt lonely and unhappy. Even Paddy was not so special to him these days. Paddy seemed to sense that Ray was not himself and appeared to try to be a good pony.

Apples, cherries, plums and currants were ripening. Garden vegetables matured faster than the family could pick them. However, much to Sampes' surprise, the city families came to the farm bringing their children for pony rides. The parents either picked their own fruits and vegetables or helped by leading Paddy as he carried their children on his back.

When the families arrived, Ray was expected to saddle Paddy. He would wink at Beaty and whisper, "Here are all your garden helpers. Keep 'em working and make sure Paddy behaves himself. That will fill our money jar a little quicker."

Paddy seemed to enjoy the experience, as the city kids fed him sugar lumps they had brought. They held out their hands hesitantly at first, as if afraid Paddy would take part of their palm along with the lump. Then they laughed with delight when Paddy lifted the lump daintily with his lips.

One boy held a bunch of carrots that had just been pulled from the garden. Paddy slowly sidled near him and quick as a wink wrenched one from the bunch. "Chomp! Crunch! Crunch!" Soon the carrot was gone and the bitter green tips were lying on the ground. Then Paddy nudged nearer for another carrot.

"No, no!" the boy said laughingly. "You can't have any more or I'll have to go back to the garden and pull some more." The children around Paddy laughed and clapped at the little show.

As the summer progressed, very little fruit and produce went to waste. This pleased the family and especially Ray, as most of the activities meant dollar signs to him. He also was pleased that Paddy was so cooperative with the children. Obviously the treats they brought for him helped alot.

Even with all these successes, Ray, on certain nights when he went to bed, felt nervous. So nervous in fact, that he tossed and turned and when he closed his eyes, the awful scene of the morning with the chickens always returned.

As he drifted off, he dreamed he was sitting in the chicken coop, among the chickens, waiting for the foxes. He had a stick to scare them away. Suddenly many foxes, too many to count, appeared at the window of the coop. Just like that the window fell in, and the foxes were in the coop with Ray and the chickens.

Ray jumped up yelling, "Get out of here," and swinging at the foxes. Chickens and feathers flew all over the coop. Ray kept swinging as he moved towards the door, but seemed to miss every time. He leaned on the door, which swung open, and out they all tumbled. Ray got up quickly and ran after the foxes, yelling, "Go away! Go away! Don't you hurt my chickens anymore!"

All of a sudden Ray felt the soft embrace of his mother's arms. He opened his eyes and Mom was soothing him and softly saying, "Wake up Ray, you've had a bad dream. I'm here and there are no foxes here." He looked around and realized that he was at the top of the stairway.

Looking at her, he said, "But I saw them and I tried to hit them with a stick, but I always missed."

Mom slowly turned Ray around and walked him back to his bed. She tucked him in saying softly, "Everything is all right. I will sit here with you until you fall asleep again."

With that, Ray rolled over and in a short time was sound asleep.

The next morning at breakfast, Mom and Dad complimented the kids about how hard they had worked. Dad said, "I think there has been too much work and not enough play for you kids, especially you, Ray. The garden has paid off. The vegetables are beating the weeds finally. Paddy's rides for the children has helped enormously with the parents picking their own fruits and vegetables."

Looking like a stern boss with a slight grin on his face, Dad declared, "After milking chores are done, you are ordered to play each evening and the duration will be for the rest of the month!"

The kids, looking at each other with funny grins, couldn't believe what they heard. The conversation quickly changed to games. Billy, always the organizer, said, "Let's play Work Up." In this game there was a batter, pitcher and a fielder. There were allotted strikeouts, with Beaty getting more. When a ball was caught on the fly in the outfield, that person would move up to pitcher and the pitcher would become the batter.

Ray liked the game "Ante, Ante Over" which involved throwing the ball over the house. That chant alerted the receiver on the other side that the ball was coming. Dad didn't care for that one very much, as every now and then a ball would end up in the rain gutter. Mom always feared for a broken window. Either way, Dad would be involved in retrieving the ball or fixing a window.

Beaty tried so hard to get the ball over the house, but just was not strong enough to do it. Ray noticed how disappointed she was and offered, "You can be the score keeper. There will be a minus for a ball landing on the roof, a point for getting it cleanly over the house and two points for catching the ball."

This suited all three just fine and they played and played until it was so dark that they couldn't see the ball anymore. A running point total for the whole month was kept on the kitchen calendar.

Ray, soon threw himself into the games. His big broad smile returned. Some evenings he saddled Paddy and went for a brisk ride over the fields.

He slept soundly from then on, his bad dreams about foxes and chickens were gone.

CHAPTER EIGHT
SUMMER'S PLAY

One Saturday, with the chicken crisis a thing of the past, Dad asked, "Whatever happened to that competition you boys were going to stage? The hay is all in the barn and we have a little time before harvesting the grain. Maybe you boys could put on a little show for us. Paddy has been such a good pony lately, it would be fun."

Billy and Ray smirked at each other and said, almost in unison, "When can we do it?"

"How about tomorrow afternoon? You two organize it." answered Dad.

The boys decided the first phase of competition would be a race, bike versus pony, on the gravel road passing in front of the house. The starting pole would be two-thirds of a mile to the left by the mailboxes. The race would end at the south corner of the front lawn, where the big oak tree would be the finish line.

The second phase of competition would be jumping. Ray asked, "Billy, how are you going to jump with your bike?"

Billy looked at Ray quizzically. "Do you remember

Jimmy Lynch at the County Fair going over the ramps, jumping parked cars and stuff? Well, I will just match your jump and land on the other side on my bike. If I fall, I lose, but you and Paddy have to jump over a pole that is the same height as my ramp."

The boys worked at their respective jumps, with Billy gathering wide planks and bricks to hold them up.

Ray finally got his side posts to stand up on their own and then looked at Billy. "Gosh, I don't know what kind of pole I can find that is light and will fall off the rests easily, so Paddy doesn't hurt himself."

Billy stood in the garage, looking around. He spotted an old bamboo fish pole. He handed it to Ray and said, "I think this will work."

Ray responded, "It's perfect. Thanks."

They practiced a little bit with their equipment behind the haybarn, as they wanted to surprise the family.

These jumps would be placed just past the porch, on the driveway leading to the road. This would give Billy and Ray ample time to stop after the jumps were completed before they got to the road. Whoever negotiated the highest jumps without falling or knocking down the pole would be the winner of the jumping segment.

The grandstand would be the long, sweeping front porch with three wide steps for sitting. Sweet smelling mock orange bushes in full bloom rimmed the porch and made the arrangement most pleasant. Mom would even offer lemonade during the show. Off in the distance to the east was the dark blue horizon line of Lake Michigan along with the steeples of several churches in the city of Manitowoc.

On race day the sun shone brightly and there was an air of excitement among the participants and spectators. Ray listened carefully to Dad's explanation of the rules of the race, while Billy just kept rocking his bike backwards and forwards, teasing Ray a little about being ready to roll. Ray noticed Paddy's ears were back, which meant he knew something different was going to happen. Ray dismounted from Paddy, rubbed his neck to calm him a little, and checked the cinch straps on the saddle to make sure they were just tight enough.

Dad said, "The winner will be whoever wins two out of three races. He will not have to do evening chores tonight."

The boys grinned at each other, because that was a nice prize.

Dad went on, "You start up by the mailboxes and I will use this little megaphone to count. One--two--three--GO and you will begin the race."

"Fair enough Dad," Ray replied with a grin, as he, on Paddy, and Billy, on his bike, slowly moved off to the mail boxes. They smiled at each other as they made their way

and turned slowly, ready for the "go" call.

Intensely they leaned forward and all of a sudden they heard Dad's "One--two--three--GO!"

Ray yelled "Giddy-up Paddy!" with a sharp kick on both sides of Paddy's ribs. Gravel flew back from his hooves. Billy also squirted stones backwards with the hind wheel of his bike. Ray kept saying, "Come on Paddy! Faster! Faster!" He and Billy were even as they approached the cherry trees just before the driveway.

Ray looked toward the porch, Dad, Mom and Beaty were standing, craning their necks. Before he knew it, he was struggling to stay in the saddle, as Paddy turned and galloped up the driveway at full speed. He grabbed the saddle horn and put all his weight on his left foot in the stirrup and righted himself as they sped past the porch. Paddy galloped right up to the door of the horse stable and stopped abruptly.

Ray upset and embarrasssed, yelled at Paddy, "What were you thinking of? We were in a race and we could have won! If you think you're going to get treats for this performance forget it and on top of that, I'm mad because I almost fell off!"

He turned Paddy around to return to the porch and there sat Billy on his bike, grinning. "I won the first race, I won the first race..." His singsong tone made Ray even madder.

"Paddy was disgusting." Ray looked at Dad and Mom. "I had no idea he would turn into the driveway."

"Well," Dad said slowly, "you know Paddy was always used to galloping up the driveway from getting the cows, not going on down the road."

"That's a poor excuse for Paddy. I didn't indicate any right turn for him. We'll fix that. I want the outside side of the road, so Billy and his bike will keep him from turning into the driveway."

As the boys returned to the mailboxes, Ray snapped a twig from the mock orange bush and stripped it of its leaves. Paddy could see the switch out of the corner of his eye and back went his ears.

"Just watch in front of you. All you will see is our rear ends all the way to the finish line Billy," quipped Ray.

They reached the mailboxes and turned around, ready for Dad's count. When "go" echoed across the countryside, both horse and bike responded with gravel flying. As they neared the cherry trees, Ray laid the switch to Paddy's backside along with a kick in the ribs. A little tug left with the reins and Paddy responded with a burst of speed and galloped right past the driveway like he forgot it was there.

Ray glanced at the porch again, Dad, Mom and Beaty were standing and yelling for each of the boys. When they reached the oak tree, there was no doubt that Ray and Paddy had won the second race.

As the boys returned to the porch, Mom said, "Maybe we should let the races end now, with each having a win."

Dad looked at the boys. "No way!" Billy protested. "We agreed it would be two out of three and that's what we're going to do."

Ray said quickly, "Sure why not?"

"That is the way it will be then," Dad said. He turned to Mom. "Where is that nice cold lemonade that was promised from our kitchen concession stand? I think the boys and Paddy should take a little rest. I"m sure Paddy would like a pail of water. He ran pretty hard in this last race. We'll all rest a bit and be ready for the final."

For the third and final race, Ray again guided Paddy to the left side of the road, away from the driveway. Ray knew they had a good start, hearing Paddy's hooves dig into the gravel. Now as they raced down the road, those little hooves digging in were like music to Ray's ears.

As they passed the porch it was a dead heat. As Billy bent over the handle bars for less air resistance, his cap flew off and his hair was flattened. Paddy's ears were back and Ray laid the switch to Paddy's backside. He also was crouching low to Paddy's neck with Paddy's long black mane almost blinding him. They looked like professional racers each to their own sport.

Dad moved to the right side of the porch and Ray, in a quick glance, knew he did that to get a better view of the finish line. It seemed like a split second and the race was over.

"Who won?" Beaty asked.

As they returned to the porch, Ray answered, "I think Paddy and I won."

"Well...ah..." Dad said thoughtfully. "It was a dead heat at the finish line as I saw it."

Ray and Billy looked at each other, grinning. Billy said, "I think we can accept that, don't you Ray? There will always be another day to try again."

"Paddy and I will look forward to that day," Ray said as he tied Paddy's reins to the porch post.

Mom got up to refill the glasses of lemonade which the boys downed very quickly. Then they scurried off to the side of the house and started setting up their ramp for Billy, and the jump bar for Paddy. They placed the jumps just past the porch, so riders would have some distance before the driveway intersected the road and the jumps were in full view of the grandstand.

Ray and Billy put the finishing touches on the jumps and Ray gathered up Paddy's reins and mounted. Mom, returning from the kitchen with more lemonade, noticed the jumps and said, "Now what is this?"

Ray responded quickly, "Listen to our announcer, Billy, and he will tell you what's coming next."

Billy started with a professional-like manner, announcing "You will now see a spectacular show similar to a Jimmy Lynch show. I will challenge gravity with a death-defying jump speeding over the eight inch ramp and landing on the other side."

He continued, "Next to me, on my right, you see Ray and his cocky Shetland pony, Paddy. They will attempt to jump over the bamboo pole suspended between the two posts. They must clear it without knocking it down, and land on the other side with Ray still on Paddy's back. Ray's jump is also eight inches high."

"Are you ready Ray?"

"Yah," Ray grinning at his audience on the porch.

Mom commented with a worried look, 'I don't know if I like this."

Dad responded, "Oh Nan, let the boys have their fun. It's their show."

With Dad's comment, Ray smiling, turned Paddy and followed Billy into the yard.

When they were ready to start, Billy yelled, "Go!" As the boys passed the house, they were going very fast. Billy zoomed up and over the ramp with no problem.

However, much to Ray's surprise, Paddy slowed when he got near the bar, stepping over it almost like a dainty lady. Watching, Dad and Mom were hysterical with laughter.

When they returned, Billy continued his Master of Ceremony's announcement, megaphone in hand. "And now the two daredevils will raise the jump four inches totaling one whole foot. Whoever gets over the jumps without a fall will be the winner! The winner's prize will be that he does not have to do his evening chores tonight."

To create more suspense, the boys circled the jumps to check if they were the same height and properly mounted. They then disappeared in back of the house to get their running start. As before, Billy and bike zoomed over the ramp, however swerving all over the driveway trying to keep in control.

This time, Paddy approached the bar at a good speed, but decided at the very last second that he was not jumping or even stepping over the bar. Paddy put on the brakes like never before, straightened his front legs, and slid up to the bar in an emphatic halt. Ray catapulted over Paddy's head in a somersault, landing on the driveway dazed but uninjured. Ray got up shaking his head. "That's the first time Paddy ever threw me."

"I made it," Billy said loudly and quickly.

"I made it over too," said Ray. "I guess you would say half of us did."

"My God," Mom broke in, "you both could have been seriously injured. Even Paddy might have stumbled. Fred, you make them stop this foolishness right now." She turned to the boys and said sternly, "You must promise never to try jumping again!"

"All right boys, you heard what Mom said. I have a tendency to agree with her. Billy, you did not have control of yourself or your bike. As Mom said, all three of you could have been injured seriously. I'm saying to both of you right now, no more jumping!"

CHAPTER NINE
THE COUNTY FAIR

The Sampe family worked hard to harvest all the grain they had planted in the spring and store the bundles in the mow, awaiting the threshing rig and crew. To separate the kernels of grain from the stalk, the crew would throw bundles out of the mow and into the rig. Out would come grain kernels on one chute, and stalks on the other. The stalks would make a giant straw stack for the kids to play in and served as bedding for the animals in the winter. Men carried bags of grain to the granary for storage in big bins. With proper timing, the family could make the most money possible on their grain crop.

The boys turned to preparing their animals for showing at the fair. Dad carefully selected a large heifer calf with good lines and stature for Billy to show in the calf competition. He told Billy that he must bond with his calf by brushing her, introduce her to a rope halter and teach her to be led slowly.

Ray had been grooming Paddy all along, so his tasks involved training him to walk, trot and canter. Dad explained to Ray that he must exaggerate Paddy's arched neck and tail, and also teach him to high-step on command.

"I'm not quite sure what you mean, Dad," said Ray.

Remember when we went to the horse show at the State Fair last year? Those show horses were trained to assume wide stances when standing still, strike the arched neck and tail pose, hold it and then subsequently move into a high stepping maneuver."

I know I can get Paddy to arch his neck by holding the reins a certain way," said Ray. "Also, I read in a book that if we bind Paddy's tail for a few weeks, the tail will arch. Thinking about Paddy lifting his hooves in the required maneuvers...how in the heck do we do that, Dad?"

"Every day, for a certain length of time, either before leading Paddy or riding him, we will tie little sandbags to his ankles," said Dad. "If he doesn't respond at first, we'll add more sand, Then as he lifts his hooves higher and higher almost like a prance, we'll lessen the sand weight until he is doing it on your command. You must develop a touch on the neck along with a special command word that will immediately put him in this maneuver. Complete control of Paddy will influence the judges greatly. Always remember to reward Paddy if he does a good job."

Ray gave Paddy treats every time he responded and improved, and the training proceeded on schedule. However, Billy preferred to do other things besides bond with his calf. Ray heard Dad warn him that the calf was rather big, and as a result, she'd be difficult to control. If and when she decided to do something other than what Billy wanted her to do, he might be in for a big surprise.

Mom and Beaty prepared for the fair too. They were making good progress on their canned vegetables and fruit, jellies and sauces. Mom had to watch that the boys didn't open her special show jars when they wanted a snack.

Dad got the job as supervisor of the poultry barn at the fair. One of his duties was to arrange cages and groupings according to the different fowl and rabbit species.

Things were going along nicely, maybe too nicely. On a warm night, both horses and cows were put out to pasture where they could graze. The horses liked this, and every now and then, being herd animals, they would take a "follow the leader" run. Of course, Paddy would run as fast as he could to keep up.

About three weeks before fair time, Ray rose early to get his practice in with Paddy. As he stepped outside, he could hear the horses whinnying. Paddy's distress whinny was louder and more repetitive than the others.

He couldn't believe his eyes when he saw Paddy trying to buck and kick against the wire gate. The big horses crowded close to him, as if trying to stop him from moving. When Ray got closer, he saw that Paddy's lower back leg was caught in the wire. The more he tried to kick, the more the barb of the wire ripped into his flesh.

Ray turned and ran back into the house, yelling up the stairs, "Dad, come quick! Paddy is caught in the barbed wire gate and is kicking and rearing, trying to free himself!"

Dad was downstairs in a flash, hurrying out to the gate. "Ray, grab Paddy's halter. Talk to him and try to calm and hold him as still as you can, while I remove the wire from his leg." Paddy seemed to know they were there to help him, and soon his leg was free. The sharp and unforgiving barbs had not only cut into his leg, but also slashed into his neck, front left chest and rear flank. All the cuts were deep and bleeding profusely.

As Dad evaluated the cuts, Ray, devastated, sank to the ground. "He won't have to be put down, will he, Dad?"

"Oh gosh no, Ray, but I don't like the looks of those gashes. And the tendon on the lower leg is nearly severed. If Paddy can make it back to the barn, tie him to his manger. Use the disinfected clothes we use for the cows' udders and try to press on all the cuts as best you can. That will stop the bleeding. I"m calling the vet right now and when I return we'll start irrigating the wounds with water.

While Paddy limped back to the barn with Ray, Dad hurried into the house and made the call. Ray tried to follow Dad's instructions. Paddy seemed to understand and stood very still.

In a short time Dad returned to the barn and reassured Ray the vet was coming. It didn't take long, and soon the vet was at Paddy's side, studying the cuts.

He turned to Ray. "You've done a good job of stopping the bleeding. However, this back leg bothers me a bit.

"The skin cuts aren't so bad, needing only a stitch or two, but the lower leg looks like the wire barb caught part of the tendon. This lower leg must be somewhat immobile until the tendon heals, requiring a tight bandage for a least a week or two, and very limited walking. Every other day you will remove the bandage and put the foot and leg in a pail of warm water and after, apply this medicine called Blue Vitriol. This will speed up the healing process and guard against infection.

"Watch now how tightly I bandage his ankle, so you will be able to do it. I'll return to check all the wounds in a week."

Ray watched as the vet shaved off the hair around the cuts and then got out a big needle syringe. The vet reassured Ray, Paddy wouldn't feel a thing. The needle contained a numbing medicine which allowed stitching Paddy's wounds. He looked at Ray with a sly smile saying, "But I'm not so sure about you."

Soon all the wounds were stitched. "There," said the vet, "I did my job and now Ray, it's up to you to do yours. I know you will do your best to bring Paddy through this unfortunate accident. You watch he will be good as new."

That evening Ray and Dad talked about Paddy. "Maybe first we should discuss just how this happened," Dad said.

"I don't think it was anyone's fault, but we must be sure it doesn't happen again.

"A severe thunder and lightning storm passed through last night, unexpectedly. There wasn't much I could do then to bring the horses in. Anyway, they usually stand quietly together and let it rain.

"A way to prevent an accident is to listen to the weather forecast for the evening. If thunderstorms are predicted, then we must keep the horses in the barn for the night.

"In this case, I think the horses panicked and ran for the gate. A flash of lightning could have been enough for the lead horse to see the wire fence and turn off. But poor Paddy, galloping behind them, ran right into it. It was just one of those freak accidents.

"We could also, I think, change the wire gate to a board gate, like the one we have entering the yard from the driveway. Horses are familiar with their exit point from a field and this kind of gate would be more visible. I think we could put it up before fair time."

Grinning and looking down at Ray, Dad said, "You know how much you boys enjoy hammering and sawing."

Ray also worked diligently to care for Paddy's injuries and the show horse training was slowed to a minimum. One day Mom came out to watch Ray working with Paddy. He went over and leaned on her. "Oh Mom, I don't know if Paddy will ever walk right. I'm afraid he won't be able to walk or trot very well in the ring. On top of that, his hair is taking so long to grow over the cuts that the judges will not think very much of him."

Mom hugged him. "Ray, don't think the worst before it happens. Knowing our Paddy, he'll show the judges a thing or two. He might not be quite one-hundred percent, but close. You run along now and encourage him to step up his gait a little without you on his back. That might gradually stretch that back leg into shape."

About a week later Mom called Ray into the house and gave him a box. "I wanted you to have these things for showing Paddy at the fair." she said with a soft, caring smile.

As he opened the box, his eyes glowed with delight. From the box, Ray pulled out a handmade bright red saddle pad. "Gee, Mom this is the best saddle pad I ever saw and this red shirt and cowboy hat trimmed in red...Paddy and I will make a dashing duo!" "Oh thank you! Thank you!"

In the meantime, Billy was trying to charm his big heifer calf, Daisy, into liking him. Finally he got Daisy to stand still while he washed and brushed her down. She finally accepted the halter on her head.

Ray watched all this, thinking Billy had a long way to go before Daisy would be ready for show. Billy tried to walk Daisy around the calf pen. Ray grinned and watched Daisy take bigger steps than Billy and push him all around. He said to Ray and Dad, "I don't think this dumb calf knows what slow lead is!"

Ray grinned all the more, but Dad got a little irritated. "That's exactly why I told you that you have to practice. Calves are not like horses and household pets that respond to commands and do it for rewards. Rewards mean nothing to a calf or cow. When they get older, they settle down."

Dad continued, "You have to get her out in the yard and make her walk slow and respond to a tug on her halter to stop so that the judges can see her lines. Take her out there in the yard and be ready to hang onto the rope."

"This I've got to see," chided Ray as he quickly ran out to the wooden yard gate to get a good, high seat for the show.

Sure enough, when they got out in the big yard, Daisy took off like a shot out of a cannon with Billy hanging onto the rope as best he could. Soon Billy let go and sank down in the middle of the yard, in pain holding his groin area.

Ray watched Daisy run wildly around and around the yard. He laughed so hard, he almost fell off the gate.

Dad, with a tinge of disgust in his voice, yelled, "Let her run, maybe that's what she wants...to run off some steam."

Billy got up ever so slowly. "You remind me of the old cowboys of yesteryear the way you're walking," Dad said. "You better go in the house and get some ice on your upper thighs. You probably pulled some muscles in your groin area and it is going to get worse before it gets better."

In the meantime, Ray's dedicated care to Paddy's injuries resulted in constant improvement and healing. Ray still was concerned about Paddy's limp, and again, he worked with the little sandbags on the ankles. Paddy had even learned the command "show" and with a quick touch on his right shoulder, Paddy strutted as best he could. He also did the stretch with front and back legs together which must have hurt a little, but Paddy held the position until Ray patted him and said "Okay Paddy."

Getting ready for the fair was a big job. Dad, Billy and Ray packed up supplies for the animals and loaded Paddy and balky Daisy into the animal trailer they had rented and off to the fair they went. While the boys busied themselves getting their animals into their stalls, Dad had crated a rooster and spring hen along with a year-old laying hen for competition. They were placed in their respective locations for judging later in the poultry house. Dad worked all day to greet the people bringing in their fowl and rabbits and placed them in cages related to their categories.

Mom and Beaty had carefully polished and labeled all the jars of preserves, along with baked goods, such as pies, cakes, cookies, bread and perfectly formed rolls. Entry tags were attached to everything. They had also pulled and picked the best matching beets and carrots with full leafed tops, cucumbers, squash and tomatoes. They chose the best and most beautiful apples, washed, and polished them until they looked waxed. It took them almost all day to place everything in their proper places and categories on the fair display tables.

The vet sought out Paddy and Ray in the pony barn that first day and carefully checked his cuts and back leg. He looked at Ray with a big smile. "Ray, you did it. Paddy has come along fine with your care." He shook Ray's hand. "Best of luck to you and Paddy on judging day."

Dad had misgivings about Billy and his Daisy, but Billy insisted they had to go to the fair and compete.

Ray whispered to Dad, "I think he just wants to be in the middle of all the fun in the cattle barn when we stay overnight to watch the animals and sleep in the hay. I'm looking forward to that myself."

The second day of the fair was judging day for animals. Ray and Paddy appeared in a special roped-off ring. Mom, watching with Dad, said, "Doesn't Ray look nice on Paddy with his outfit and the red saddle pad? Paddy's coat shines like patent leather shoes." Ray heard his Mom as he passed by them. He knew he and Paddy were making a good presentation. Paddy's long, full tail had responded to the binding and he arched his neck in response to the way Ray held the reins. The judges put all the ponies through their paces of slow walk, trot and canter. Ray whispered to Paddy, "You are doing just fine...keep trying to lift that back leg."

The presenters were asked to remove their pony's saddles and the judges moved in much closer to check back lines, shoulders and flanks for firmness. The judge even checked Paddy's teeth and hooves.

Another walk around the circle and then three Shetlands were picked for a final discussion amongst the judges. One was Paddy! Ray smiled proudly at the judges and his family. Then the judges announced they had made their decisions.

They picked a little black and white Shetland first, Paddy second and another brown pony third. Ray's smile disappeared as he looked at his red ribbon. His eyes filled with tears, but he quickly brushed them away so his family wouldn't notice. Thoughts of all the work...he believed made Paddy the best-trained pony flashed through his mind. He was so disappointed that Paddy didn't win first prize.

As Ray left the ring looking down, one of the judges stopped him. "Young man, you have one of the best Shetland specimens I have seen in a long time. But with the uneven gait and some scars, we had no choice but to award first to the other pony. What the heck happened to him anyway?" asked the judge.

Ray responded quickly, "A couple of weeks ago he ran into a barbed wire fence during a storm."

"Well that certainly was unfortunate. Bring that little guy back next year, and if he doesn't hurt himself again, he'll take first for sure."

The judge's comments made Ray feel much better. He waved his red ribbon to his family and led Paddy back to the horse barn.

That afternoon, cattle judging began with the heifer calves. The family went to eat a quick lunch at a food stand which was between the cattle ring and the carnival midway. Ray ate his lunch very quickly as he wanted to get back to watch Billy and see how he and Daisy were getting along.

Daisy stood quietly for the final brush down and then when Billy put the scratchy rope halter on Daisy, she made it quite clear that she didn't like it. Ray stood there grinning watching both Billy and Daisy getting frustrated with each other.

The announcement echoed through the cattle barn. "All heifer calf competition should approach the show ring!" Ray quickly took a place by the ring with a good vantage point. All the people stood cheering for their respective sons, daughters, brothers and sisters and their show animals. This was the biggest class of competition for all livestock being shown at the fair.

Daisy took one look around and bolted toward the crowd, leaped over the ring rope, with Billy holding on with all his might. People yelled and scattered. As the commotion of an out-of-control Daisy and Billy headed towards the Midway, Ray followed as close as he could, but never got close enough to help Billy.

As they reached their family eating at the stand, Dad craned his neck to see what made the crowd yell and run towards them. "Oh my gosh! Daisy is completely out of control!"

They went by so quickly that Dad was unable to stop Daisy. Ray stopped running and threw his hands up in despair.

"Poor Billy," Ray said to Dad. Right then Billy's legs gave out and he went splat, headfirst, still hanging on to the rope with the dust coating his face and shoulders. "Boy, that didn't even slow Daisy down any," Ray said.

Now there was only a small distance between Daisy and Billy and the crowds of children and parents around the rides of the Midway. A large burly man was watching children on the rides when he noticed Daisy, dragging Billy, headed directly at him. He side-stepped a bit and as they passed him, Billy let go of the rope in utter exhaustion. The man immediately stepped on the trailing rope. That stopped Daisy with the whip of her head and she stood almost upright for a few seconds. The man gathered in the rope and held her by her halter. She was unable to move.

Billy looked so funny with his face full of dirt and dust, even on his eyelashes, which made him look even funnier. His eyes were big as saucers, looking up at the big man, Billy in a state of shock. "Ah...ah...ah..." He struggled to his feet and said, "Gee thanks for stopping her. She kind of got away from me."

Ray stood next to Billy with a half-grin. "That's the understatement of the year, but it was quite a show." The man smiled and said softly, "Glad I could help, young man."

Billy thanked the man again and murmured to the crowd around him several times, "I'm sorry."

Dad thanked the man too. "I think I will take over from here." He walked Daisy back to the barn with a firm hand.

Ray just couldn't let the moment pass without a few more comments. Laughingly, he said to Billy, "Thank goodness that guy was as big as he was. Maybe he should show Daisy instead of you."

Billy walking along, shaking his head. "All she had to do was walk around the ring slowly. What a dunce she made of me."

Of course, Billy was disqualified as his heifer calf "failed to appear." As they rode home, Dad said to Billy, "A lesson learned, and you better get the old ice packs out again." He smiled a little. "The main thing...no one was hurt."

"Well, except me," Billy replied rubbing his thighs.

When fair week ended, the Sampe family had gotten many firsts, including Dad's chicken entries. But Mom and Beaty with their multitude of entries made the most prize money with all their "firsts." Ray, though, was still very proud, as Paddy's red ribbon paid four dollars. The red ribbon itself represented a dedicated effort on Paddy's behalf. He smiled ear to ear as he added that to the money jar which was full almost to the top. He was sure that soon Paddy would be all his.

CHAPTER TEN
THE GREAT CHASE

FINAL ACCOUNTING

Summer was drawing to a close and the boys knew that soon school would start. That meant that some big final jobs would have to be done. One was quite apparent, as they casually glanced at the pig pen accompanied by the strong odor, that would be one of them. After several cleanings, hopefully this would be the last time and then the pigs would be gone.

The piglets had grown big and strong with unusually long legs. Ray remarked to Billy, "You know if those two ever got loose, we might have a big chase to get them back in the pen."

The next morning at breakfast, Dad smiled at the boys. "Well, boys, the pigs have grown into fine porkers and today will probably be the last time you will have to clean the pen."

With long faces, Ray and Billy slowly trudged towards the barn, as Beaty ran along side, grinning, holding her nose and mimicking the boys' expressions. Billy turned to Ray and said, "We have to have our kid sister teasing us about the blasted job on top of everything else. God, I hope this is the last time!"

"Just keep it up," Ray said in a threatening voice to Beaty, "and you're going to get it!"

Ray and Billy worked furiously to pile the muck by the door so it could be loaded and hauled away. As the boys worked to get the distasteful job done, Beaty kept lurking around the door. At times she opened it just an inch or two to smile at them, which frustrated them even more. Ray warned her, "Don't open the door too far!"

On one peek, Beaty didn't notice that one of the pigs was close to the door. When the pig saw light it jumped, pushing its snoot through the opening and knocking Beaty down. Just like that two lively pigs were romping around in the yard.

The boys stood there for a moment, dumbfounded that the pigs moved so quickly. Ray turned to Beaty, "Now see what you've done. They are tough little buggers to catch. Look how fast they can run. You better stick around to help us get them back in the pen."

As the three started after the pigs, Ray yelled, "The pigs are out! The pigs are out!"

Finally Dad heard Ray's cries. He approached the boys with his hands on his hips, looking stern.

"We didn't do it," Ray yelled, "Beaty let them out!"

"Never mind who let them out. The important thing

is to get them back in the pen," Dad ordered. Then Mom came out.

"Mom!" Ray said, "Can you help us corner the pigs by the barn and silo?"

In the meantime, the pigs were having the time of their lives, running, leaping, darting and squealing around each other and the boys.

"Okay now," Dad said. "Let's gradually maneuver them into the corner by the silo. We'll move in slowly, closing the circle. You Ray, Billy and Mom stay close to me and I will grab at least one of them as it tries to get past. The other will probably follow and you can grab that one."

As the family closed in and Dad was almost ready to grab one of the pigs, they veered suddenly.

"Oh gosh," Dad remarked. "You might know they would go for our weakest link in the circle. Beaty! Watch it! They're headed towards you. Try not to let them through."

The pigs ran straight for Beaty. Ray knew by the frightened look on her face that she would panic. "Wave your arms or something to stop them!" yelled Ray.

But Beaty held her arms up to her chest and turned sideways. There was a little space on either side of her, and the pigs saw it and scooted right past her and started down the driveway.

Dad turned to Ray. "Quickly Ray, bridle Paddy. He's

in the barn. Ride bareback and take Teddy with you. Try to head them off and get them back here!"

Quick as a flash, Ray was in Paddy's stall, yanking the bridle over the startled pony's head. "Paddy, we're gonna chase pigs," Ray said hurriedly.

He threw himself on Paddy's back and ducked his head as he went through the barn door. "Giddy-up Paddy and come on Teddy!"

The pigs were almost to the first hill when Ray and Paddy kicked up the turf passing over the front lawn. When they got on the road, the stones flew from Paddy's hooves. Teddy barked and Paddy's notrils flared, ears back as they barreled down on the pigs at full speed. Ray felt his hair flatten on his head. When he, Paddy and Teddy caught up with them, the pigs scattered into the deep grass-filled ditches.

Ray and Paddy leaped into the ditch in front of one pig, but he jumped out and ran across the road to join his buddy in the other ditch. Ray and Paddy leaped onto the road and then plunged into the ditch on the other side, Ray almost losing his balance. However the elusive pigs continued crossing back and forth.

Ray was glad that Teddy was along. He noticed that Teddy tried to turn the pigs toward home. The grass was so deep in the ditches that Teddy had trouble seeing the pigs. At least Teddy's sharp bark helped confuse them so they did not know just where the dog was. When the pigs darted across the road, Ray yelled, "Over here Teddy, get 'um!"

Ray noticed that at the bottom of the second hill, the pigs were struggling onto the road. "Aha! You're finally tired." Ray muttered as he maneuvered himself slowly with Paddy and Teddy between the pigs and busy Federal Highway 10.

Highway 10 curved at the intersection with the Sampes' road, which did not allow drivers much time to react if they saw an obstruction. Traffic sped along this highway, because it was the main highway from the northwest leading into Manitowoc and to the Lake Michigan shoreline. Losing control could send a vehicle down into the ravines on either side of the intersection.

Ray knew the pigs must not reach the highway, and he, Paddy and Teddy stood defiantly, challenging the pigs. After staring at each other, the pigs slowly turned and started back up the hill toward the farm. Relieved, Ray grinned and thought... we won!

As they approached the house, Ray was surprised to find the family clapping and hailing him as the victor. "We watched you all the way down the road," Dad commented. "You displayed great horsemanship to be able to stay on Paddy with the leaps in and out of those deep ditches."

By now the pigs were thirsty, hungry and slowly approached their open pen door. As they jumped back into the pen, Beaty ran up and slammed the door shut. She turned, sheepishly leaning on it with a sly grin.

Although they were all happy with how the pig chase

turned out, Ray knew that Dad wasn't too happy about how they got out in the first place. He admonished Beaty for opening the pig pen door. "Now you see what can happen. Thank goodness we have our pigs and our heroes in one piece and no car accidents down on the highway. We will all look forward to pork roasts roasting in the oven with the mouth-watering smell filling the kitchen."

Before they knew it, fall was upon them with bitter cold winds piling up old dried leaves in the corners of the buildings and the grass turning brown. Most of the birds had left for warmer places. The warm kitchen with its wood stove became an inviting place for the family to gather.

The last of the season's work had been completed. The stored hay and grain were now being enjoyed by the animals and chickens. The last of the squash, pumpkins and apples were stored in the basement along with all the wonderful jellies, jams and sauces.

Ray and his family talked and reminisced about all the things that had happened, some serious, like the chicken disaster and Paddy's accident and vet bill, and others humorous, like the races and Billy's outing with Daisy at the fair. Ray remarked, "Then those pigs...Paddy deserves most of the credit for avoiding a disaster. And now we can look forward to pork roasts and chops that didn't cost much other than the feed."

Mom and Dad got out the accounting books and spread them out for the children to see. They showed them basic costs of feed and resulting rewards from the sale of milk, grains, vegetables, fruit and chickens. Billy and Ray enjoyed adding up the prize money. Ray couldn't resist pointing out that his Paddy had won four dollars, whereas Daisy "failed to appear." The whole family laughed for a long time remembering that episode.

Beaty was sitting there watching and listening when Ray said to her, "You can dump out the jar from the pantry and put dollar bills in one pile, and coins according to size in other piles. It will be easy for us to add them up then." The clinking of the coins was music to Ray's ears as Beaty worked.

Dad remarked, "Boy, not only did we stay off county assistance, but we are able to meet the last payment for Paddy. We even have a little left over for a movie or some other fun."

Beaty, leaning her chin on her hand, comically said with raised eyebrows, "Next summer, could we make a smaller garden?" They all laughed at her remark knowing what she really meant to say was smaller garden/less work.

Ray, grinning from ear to ear, stood up. "Jeepers, thanks to all of you...you helped Paddy join our family and I know our funny, quirky pony will give us many fun times in the future."

"And now," trying to be as tall as he could and squaring his shoulders, said, "I just have to go out to the barn and give Paddy a big hug, 'cuz he's mine!"